TALES FROM THE DARTRY MOUNTAINS

TALES
FROM THE
DARTRY MOUNTAINS

Poems

Charlie Gracie

diehard poetry

Diehard Poetry at the Callander Press,
91–93 Main Street, Callander, Scotland
FK17 8BQ

Design and typesetting by Gerry Cambridge
gerry.cambridge@btinternet.com

ISBN 978-1-913106-52-2

Printed by Imprint Digital, Exeter
www.digital.imprint.co.uk

Diehard
Scotland and Cumbria

Contents

The Purpose of Poetry

To lead you up the Dartry Mountains
and there to hear a lark in the spiral air.

To know the beauty of the bog, the soft squish of moss.

To lighten your eyes
to liven your ears
to press home a point about love.

To hold you still.

To give a voice to the darkening wind
a voice, to the south, of danger
to the north, of presence
to east and west, of eternity
as it whispers
so you cannot hear.

* *For McGloins Everywhere* *

The Dartry Mountains run from Benbulben
in County Sligo north to Arroo that overlooks
Lough Melvin. My mother was born among these
mountains in the town land of Magheramore,
Glenade. This is border country: Lough Melvin is
run through with a dotted line that marks the join
between Fermanagh and Leitrim, the UK and Eire,
Ulster and Connacht.

McGloins

Did they come, these offspring of Eoghan
from the land, the Tír, of Eoghan?

Did they take the offer of Connacht
rather than the threat of Hell?

Did they trudge from Cromwell's guns
to the boggy soak of Largydonnell?

Did they leave lush land
land and homes, land and homes and beasts?

Did they shed quiet tears on the road
and hold the childer tight in?

Did they weep again in bog-soaked Leitrim
in the wet Leitrim bog?

Did they close their eyes and pray in Connacht's green
pray for their childer's childer?

Did they chill their bones in the wet soak of Glenade
let the wet soak seep into their hearts?

Did they fight the inevitability of failure
and rise, generations later, to hold their heads up?

The Gun

There was a gun in Glenade and they had it. Alice never liked it
when it was there, snuggled in a thatch in the shed. But
you had to take your turn and keep it out the hands of the Brits.

If the Black and Tans found it, the whole family would be shot.
She'd heard tell of a thing like that up beyond Belcoo,
a father and a mother and a child.

But they had to take their turn.
For the sake of the boys and our sake too, said Daddy,
his brother a captain and all.

She heard them tearing up Annie Rooney's.
Sounded like plates smashed and her baby crying,
Frankie out against the wall to keep him tight.

Jesus, they're fuckers, she whispered to herself,
when Mammy told her to hide the gun better.
If they find it here we're done for.

But a girl of eighteen summers, with the fear upon her,
the gun in her hand and them coming over the two fields,
and nothing now to do but run back to Mammy.

Too late to be safe, but a mammy is a quick thinker,
and the gun is in the milk churn, half full,
and it might give them half a chance.

They're in, tearing up the wattle and emptying the drawers,
Daddy pinned against the back wall like Frankie was,
Mammy saying damn all, and the churn untouched.

And after, in the late light,
Mammy will laugh.
Squeeze Alice tight.

Black and Tans

He hit her out the bed with the rifle butt.
Seven months, she was, heavy with the first of her childer,
heavy in heart too, she was,
when she'd heard them yelling at the door,
English voices, and her there alone.
'The guns, ya Fenian bitch.'
She was glad it was just the guns he was after,
her lying there in her bed,
Paddy out late in the field beyond with Frankie Rooney.

There were three men in the room, all breathing hard,
and the sweat of war still upon them.
She wondered then how old the one at the back was,
maybe her own age, with his fresh face.
He didn't look at her,
worked away at the wattle with the bayonet.

She picked herself from the floor. 'We've no gun.'
She wanted to scratch at them,
get her strong right hand to them,
but she prayed that Paddy would not come in,
get shot for his anger,
like happened the Osborne boy in Carrick.
Jesus, his mother must be sore with that.

As quick as they'd burst into the room, they left,
wisps of their breath still in the air.
She watched them slink to the next house along.
Annie would get it now.
The young man turned, his face dark.
His eyes, in the evening light, shone a little.
He tried a smile, but it didn't come.
She set her own face firm, thinking of the boy inside her belly,
hoped no mother would see him like that.

Magheramore to Bundoran Flit

The donkey is not for shifting.
She stands full square at the road end, face out
to the bright sea, the cart behind her laden with
everything we have:
beds,
accoutrements,
pots, pans,
the four smallest childer,
table and chairs.
The childer shouting, 'Move yer arse, donkey.'
Nothing, her head in that head down donkey way.
And we're done in from pulling and pushing her,
walking all the day from Magheramore.
Nobody said a word from the Glenade Church
till the smiddy at Kinlough, a silent trudge
to some kind of a new life.

Now, in bright Bundoran light,
all we need is for this fecker to turn right.
Hughie Travers and four men
drunk in Doherty's door
'Kick the fecker in the head.'
'Give it a carrot.'
'Kick the fecker up the arse.'

Paddy and them, they take the weight
of the donkey like taking the weight
of a coffin. They lift. Shuffle round.
The donkey snorts. Wee Jimmy cries.
The men skiff their feet on the dust of the road.
The donkey turns slowly.
She snorts again, and off we go
to the new house.
Hughie Travers, in the dimming night,
'That's a pint ye owe us, ya Leitrim Boy.'

Going Back to Saint Bridget's Terrace

Every summer, we stepped off the Glasgow bus
into the choke of turf smoke and the click of jackdaws.
You can smell the sea from there, salt in the wind.

On the walk up to Granny's
Carmel Barry, with her happy 'Welcome home'
then Granny, at the door of the house, kitchen cloth in her hand
the smell of eggs and potatoes, a tearful hallo.

It's gone now, the house
renovated beyond recognition.
But she is still there, bow-legged on the doorstep
her tight mouth waiting to welcome me.

Beyond the fields, Arroo Mountain sets it face to the sea.

Jackdaws

It is this with jackdaws.
They were squeezed into peat bogs,
their beaks and bones and feathers and blood
left to seep into the soft ground.
They floated in the semi-hard earth
then eased their bodies into each another,
until, with the wood of the trees, the filaments of grasses,
the crushed bodies of beasties and deer and people,
they became the earth.

Jackdaw's souls never leave their bodies.
They ooze all their black godliness into their molecules
 and wait.
When I burn turf, the essence of jackdaws smears the
 chimney walls,
glistening blackly in the black soot.
They rebirth from the embryonic dark, from the smear of soot
then clamber, clicking and glossy, into the late spring air.

The smell of burning turf is the smell of a jackdaw's birth.

Kate

a black-haired ghost on the very edge of memory
she always said hallo, how are ye, in a ringing voice
walked into the sea one day
nobody knew why

The Thing the Curlew Does

half-wheep
half-wheep while it builds to the fullness of
its slow ululation

the sky and everything it has
stills
the song
fills all the space there is.

On Benbulben

Ancient

the chortle call of choughs
flickering out over peat hags
fairies in the bog-lit mountain

Civil War

A step from Bulben to Wiskin
to something un-named
hands wrung, blood-saddened

Meadow Pipit

A swirl-chirp blurring above
the height of the mountain. Silence
blasts out below

Yeats

In the green expanse of Sligo
a river wanders through
the footprints of ancient forts.

Leaving

Behind you, beyond the whins
a Council of Crags
in the softening sun

Memorial

A cross there to five poor cunts that got killed in the Civil War.
Runnin off the back of Benwiskin, on the Glencarr side,
runnin for their lives they were,
only to be hemmed in
on the boggy top
and gunned down.

Near the end of the war too
near the end of the whole fuckin thing.

On Benwisken

Rocks, grass, sphagnum. A drizzled scatter of crows
in the multi-grey sky, black to grey-black to all the softness
of greys, and the whitened edges of clouds.

Sun wetly threatened in distant pale blue.

The pink shell of a mountain snail.

Tiny white star of Pearlwort.

How to Get to a Secret Lough

The road from Glenade church and up past the houses there.
The farmers have signs to say keep out and private road and
the like. Ignore them. Tell them you're a McGloin and you'll
be fine. It's a bad road, pot-holed and half patched and worse
the more you go. Just beyond the last of the brambles, heavy
with un-ripened fruit, a gate that you'll hardly be able to open
without farmer's arms. Jump over that and spludge in the
mud, it's the best way. Then, every tree and bush is gone, it
is land now for sheepshite and grass. What track there is, is
gravelly, the nature grabbing back charge. It is hard to find
the Green Road, but that's what you need to do. It is a thing
you breathe in, rather than locate, a thing you'll know you're
at when you're there. The track: now that would wind and
wind you round and get you lost in the far glen. Work your
legs, up and up the scree. That'll be you on the Green
Road, the road to the crags. There's hardly a space between
them for a one to get to the top of the mountain, hardly a
crack in their black teeth to let you through. But somewhere,
when you are right tight under them, you'll see the way. The
green flat top of the mountain flops over and winks, come
on boyo.

In one place, in all the cragginess,
there is a space for you to climb.
And once you've climbed, to sit.
To sit in the softness of heathery moss.
Moss and heather and the wind that flies off the sea.
The sea in the distance, with Saint John's Point beyond,
and the wildness of Mullaghmore.

You can sit there and love it all. Then, not to dally long for
the fear of hill mist, you tread large steps, the ups and downs
of boggy land are such that you need to do that. Little steps
don't work here. Cut round the edge of the mountain, the
black crags now invisible to you. There is no direction to go
except around the mountain. The ups and downs of it. The
edge of it to follow. Truskmore, Tievebaun, they appear,
their now distant green above their own crags, sweeps of
moss and rock. The lough, a lochan I call it in my
Scottishness, is not anywhere up here until it appears, sudden
as sunshine, in a glimpse beyond the rise of heather and bog
cotton. From the corner of my eye it is, then gone as soon as
I make over to it. There it's back now, a real thing, a faerie
breath of a thing, a geological and pluvial creation. It sits in
the shallow cradle of Arroo Mountain. The far end meets the
sky. Then nothing but distant Leitrim hills.

sky reflected in flat calm
a fly buzzes in cotton grass
I lie here and sleep

Border

...up the side of Lough Melvin
from Kinlough to Garrison
then to Belcoo and
back to Blacklion over the simplest of bridges
weaving in and out of
Euro and Pound
country and country
province and province

The Bradan Road

Between Omagh and the way to Belleek,
you turn off to take the Bradan Road,
one of those drumlinned ribbons
that bounce through green parcels of land.

I'm thinking that Bradan might easily become Broughton,
imagining the Irish turn of the sound of
the a shape into a drawling *au*,
and the thing we both do,
us Irish and us Scots,
the softening of a *d* to *t*.

Mammy on a Chopper

My bike's a purple Chopper
but Mammy takes it every day,
rides up to Barlanark, up to her work at Pendeen,
in her sheepskin coat
and a headscarf.
It's a pure rid neck
as she wobbles in the first two turns of the wheels,
then shouts a Yeehaa!
when she gets going right and fires off.

She'd have run about the fields in Magheramore barefoot
and up the steep sides of Gortnagarn,
skiting her toes on rocks.
The boys washed at the outside tap
while she, with curtains closed for modesty,
washed at the kitchen sink.
So now it seems obvious to use what is at hand
To go to work on a Chopper
to save a bit for a better cut of meat.

Other Poems

Frogs Mating & Isabel Mowing

This sound poem was recorded on a late spring morning in Thornhill on the edge of the Trossachs.

Scan the QR code to listen or go to
https://bit.ly/2BpeDpV

Huge thanks to musician and sound artist Tom Dalzell for editing the piece.

soundcloud.com/lives-as-omens

facebook.com/tomdalzell2

In Blanchland

in the square there is nearly nothing
the post office, a deli, the closed doors of houses
Pennine stone frames everything
in this hardly peopled place
visitors hide in the White Monk, eating broth

in late smoky sunshine, hollyhocks breathe their last
ranks of gardens squeeze final inches of growth
leeks, the skeletal ends of sunflowers, blooded haws
the walls of the houses are warm

over the field to the river
past sagging washing,
one side sun-drying, the other frosted
in the dark stretch of trees, the river skips
over brown stones
oak, ash, beech lean over,
drinking from the wet rush

a pine on the bridle path, high and soft barked
we hug, the soft-barked tree and me
talk in hush about all things since we last met
the school closed
the Consett works too
the football field was flattened and drained
my father died
on Bale Hill new trees were sowed
and in squished-in houses
fire upon fire upon fire laid and spent in front rooms

Across the Fold

(found poem, *Belfast Telegraph*, April 2018)

GOOD FRIDAY AGREEMENT, 20 YEARS ON
UDA to announce they are relinquishing crime
New poll: 51% more likely to have pals of same religion
Powell: some unionists prefer Irish unity to Brexit
Coveney: anniversary will focus minds on future
Adams: unionism lacks the leadership it had in 1988

Photograph:
street of terraced houses,
a straggle of police tape,
an officer of the law
BELFAST MURDER
TWO HELD AFTER
DEATH OF MAN

Ungrasped

Scotland, 19 September 2014

the boil of a fish rising in Loch Barvas
a face, a child at the steamed bus window
silvering of mist, soft on the morning road
your brown eyes, held for a moment too long
a balloon let go from a child's hand
my heart in a flutter

horizon, obscured in cloud

The Ghost of Alan Hiney in Barga

We sat in early morning brio at Bar Alpino
as the ghost of my friend wandered on the chattering roadside.

Everything around me stilled,
the yatter smoothed into nearly nothing,
the smell of cigarettes and coffee misted.

I let myself drift into his face.
The turn of his mouth.
His eyes looking right into the very middle of me.

I made this ghost be him,
my friend who drank and laughed me half to death,
who breathed my air with me.

He moved me again
for a moment
on the roadside.

In Rottenmann

The lassie behind the counter in the Stadtcafé is Turkish.
'Haben Sie glutenfrei Brot?'
I've practised it. Meine Frau ist glutenfrei.
I scrabble in my dictionary for sandwich —
it's the same word.
She uses Google for the choice of fillings.

She has not heard of Scotland.
I explain that it's a country north of England.
A different country.
I think she understands. 'Ist gut,' she says.

Her name is Ala.
We have a photograph of her
standing outside the café with meine Frau,
smiling into the white heat of the Austrian summer.

A Photograph of Our Father

Backlit on his chair
he leans forward into the room,
black and brimming white, he is alive.
You took that photograph,
set the camera quietly.
He was unaware you were even there.

The afternoon light split the window.
Such a strong light
that very near blanched him,
left a shadowed impression.
His hand reaches for a cup on the table,
the one we got from Granny's house.
He took his tea black.

It was a Saturday.
I lay on the sofa,
out of shot, chatting to him.
Talked about nothing.
I watched you set up
adjust the stops
check the framing was perfect.
Then the click
that made him turn to you
and smile.

For Better

I would never have hoped to wipe his backside
or comfort him like his mammy might

never have hoped that he, once boyish and tall
would become this un-sparked life
that all my lust would douse itself
that I would be nothing like a wife

never have hoped to meet the end of love

in our quiet moments late at night
we promised that our passion would be
the last thing we breathed out

What I've Learned About Love

We folded it into all we did
children, house-painting, holidays.
Seeded it blindly.

Then love moved its feet
tipped, impolitely, over the thin line.

So how
it seems impossible to know
does this arise?
You, from the corner of my heart
fierce, flamed.
Eager and suddenly everything.

Old Skin

I can offer you this old skin
bumps and scrapes
less smooth than if we had met when young

I wonder how many times we nearly did
skip past each other in the swimming baths
sit a train seat apart, freshly spruced for the Sub Club

new skin then, hardly out the wrapper
big eyes taking the whole world in

this old skin wrinkles under my touch
that scar on my back from the doctor's knife
the one on my head when I fell drunk up the Brig
it covers bones that creak more than I like

old skin is less tentative, disinclined to freeze
it has learned to stretch, knows its limits

I could tell you a million stories about this skin

Uncle Charlie

Charles Gracie left Belfast in the summer of 1910.
He took a boat to the Broomielaw
and never went back again.

He was Uncle Charlie, a man built for the pits
a man for the howk and pull, in the deep dark.
We love him, this unknown ghost
who walked in the shadowed side of our family,
cast smiles into hearts.

I wonder who we would have now at weddings, funerals.
Cousins and aunties and uncles from this man,
great warm hugs, drunken nights, generations of Gracies.

Waiting For an Autumn Grandchild

These are the hours before you arrive
in breath to our little cave of space and time.
The leaves on birch trees have turned,
and the slime of death is already on the ground
on this lazy-rain day.
It is not a bad or a sad thing, this slimy death,
no more than your birth will be
the best thing that has ever happened.

You are
the centre of your and my world
at this and every moment,
and a nothing of soon-to-be-dead dust
cluttering up the tiniest of universal spaces.

Love, always.

The Da

Dinner was cooked by my (fair) hand
then dishes, cutlery, pots abandoned.

'If you end up leaving them,
we'll do them when we get back.'

Almost gratefully
my hands are immersed in suds
Da
cook, washer-upper, New Man
the father of daughters, unleashed
equal.

Wid

When Bob Hendry was a boy
Saint John's Wid was filled with ash and birch.
His faither and him
they caught deer on straw-tied butcher hooks
hung a hook on a birch branch
for a beast to grab and strand on,
its back legs tip-toing
dribbled with blood
on the soft moss.

After the war they scraped the deciduous life away,
filled the airy space with larch and spruce
a sparse dark death of a wood.

And now, the open wound of harvest
nothing but the stubble of trunks

Time.
For a new planting.

Gatehouse Crow

A thing of deep dark blue
all the power of sun and earth
in its jump, crouch, flap.

And suddenly
in a turn to the light
it is matt black, flat and almost nothing.

How is this
this change
this flip from form to phantom?

Gate

sing the sky on Stronend
strums in a big air
the wheep of oystercatcher

the sinew steel of a gate
pulses the middle field
soft wave of verge grass

hands fold on the bar
into a wild wet land
bleat of lamb

Early December, Moniack

A flurry of fieldfares in green emptiness.
Grey layers of sky holding back on everything
but the tiniest flickers of snow.

Nothing has quite died yet,
whins poke tiny yellow eyes into the empty wind.

Coldoch Broch, as Birds Consider Coupling

The declamation of crows in late winter
is languid, a flaccid cry
too early to be more than aspiration.
And I'm lying here
on a weakening February day
on curled beech leaves, holding myself
only just together.

Wren

she is here, le roitelet
the wee king, gærdsmutte
creeps in the shadows
in her undergrowth cave
she is a grey-brown thing
among grey-brown stuff
can't see me
can't see me
can't see me
the wren is the king of the hedge
Zaunkönig, they say in German
king of the liminal
she sits, this king of her own space
in her tininess, launching fierce
shouts into the afternoon air
I am here
I am here
I am here

We Reclaimed Strath Rannoch

in bleaching February sun
we swept Mitsy's Forest for enemies
placed our mark on John Coyle Rock
secured the river crossing at Picnic Bridge

in the distance, Seana Bhraigh held its own line
and we trawled dark shimmers of pools
late light of winter on our backs

we ate in the bright snowy blast of noon

each woman, each man, each child, each dog
we held our breath
for a moment then
in the rustle of glen
the sudden cold of treeshade
the spate rush of snowmelt

Lennoxtown, Summer

There is more than dust at the side of this road.
The thrown-away thrive here,
flapping in the starling-sheen of puddles.

Royston Kirk, Whose Steeple Alone Remains

Above disassembled stones
incongregate prayers
a spire, crossless
touches nothing
neither in heaven nor on earth.

Hut

I like the rain brutal, the nights dark
they hardly come here then
just the occasional drib of human

on days when the sun warms the air
they vomit their children
into the picnic blanket car park
let the wind blow the smell of streets away
shout out to the big land below

they rise, a swirl-sump
of
mammies and daddies and grannies and weans
on the scrape of grass, to the top of the brae
the children rub their knees bloody on my skin
climb on me, scrabble inside
smell the smell of pish in my corners

on stagnant nights their young shag inside me
spark up joints and spark cans
squeeze tits and hold hands
they giggle and snog, fashion dreams
that might be nothing but impossible

I like the rain brutal, the nights dark
just the occasional drib of human
happy to be alone

The Poet Reads His Poem

It's been a marriage, he says, of nearly forty years
and doesn't have to smile down to his wife
for everyone to know that if he did
it would be warm.

She blanches with the unnecessariness of it
and glances at the seat he had occupied
before he took to the stage and read his poems
until this poem
where he unfolds the intimacy of those decades
in the delicacy of paper
the fineness of memories
the beauty of his wife.

When he ends the poem, he does smile, a wee smirk
and she returns a comic castigation
with a twist of her lips and a lowering of her brow.

Tiny movements honed year on year to these things
the smirk a man gives his wife
to tell her all the love he has
the twist of a woman's lips and the shift of a brow
to meet him there.

A Poet at the Lake

I took Chrys Salt to the lake today.
We'd a great time, sitting in the Jura sun
tres, mais pas trop, chaud.
She whispered to me
light your lanterns Charlie.

We sat on the grass at Lamoura.
I soaked in the sploosh of her words,
breathed in the warm air
All Wind, all of it,
smelled the sweat as she worked.

When I swam, she sat there, waiting,
(a poem never rests, you know, always un-still),
then alive again, yelling, stamping feet.
We ate ice cream, and it mattered.
It really did.

Unravelling with Martha Wainwright

Martha welled up on stage
rage contained, she shed light
cast her words on the blur of the crowd

we stood at the far wall, unintimate
pricked by the beauty of her voice

in front of us, a straggle of backs
stray hands in waistbands
and on soft-haired necks
the occasional kiss swaying
in the swoon of her pain

after, in the late city light
we looked deeply at each other
closely
right the way in
tried to push back
the unstoppable squeeze of sadness

The Basket Maker

She is where beauty lives
in the tightening angles of arm, hand, finger
her eyes fixed, lips pressed
breath definite, slow.

She smells of the earth.
Not the willowy sweet
or the fulsome green.
Hers is the elemental earth
the earth of fire, bubbling unseen
of stones, ground to nearly nothing
where seeds will lie for aeons.

She has the tough hands of a god
a god of the dark deep
muscles shapes from dried weeds
nothing they can do now but yield
nothing they can do but wait
for what she will make of them

Howson's Ogilvie

St Andrew's Cathedral, Glasgow

He is hung on the wall of the side chapel,
larger than any life.
Not a bit of saintly certainty in his eyes,
he reaches beyond the watchers.

John Ogilvie.
Unblessed.
Unsanctified.

He stands on the hot coals of his undoers and
leans his neck into the noose,
the tormented Paradise behind him
all his nothingness clasped between his fingers.

Ye Dancin?

Barga, in summer sun, and I've polished up my Italian.
'Una birra alla spina, per favore.'
'That a pint or a hauf pint, pal?'
A husky resonance of the Clyde.

She has old skin, but her eyes sparkle, soft and brown.
Her parents, refugees from dry Tuscan hills
to the bright, damp hope of Troon.
She married a McLean, lost her Moscardini tag,
but not her Moscardini heart.
Now, no husband or bambini in Scotland any more,
she is a nonna here.

'Do you miss it?'
'I miss,'
she takes her husband's ghost in the pose,
'a dance on a slidey floor,'
and turns, as light on her feet as she always was.
'The Gaiety, where I met my Bill.
He took me to Francie and Josie the very next week.
'Ye dancin?'
'Ye askin?'
'Ah'm askin...'
She laughs a long wheeze.
'Bill hated them. A couple of eejits, he said.'

She grabs him again and spins off,
a waltz in dusty sunbeams

Hospital Tea Break

the tiny space alive with smoke and the chat of women
you don't get fucked when you're over fifty
laughs, swigs of tea, long draws on fags
I focus on the floor, redden to the tune of their voices
Ah think Ah've become a virgin again
eyes burn into my head

I can feel their sweat,
inhale it with the smoke, slurp it with my tea
sweet sweat, worked up in a morning
of lifting and changing and feeding
makes me want
to be a woman,
to laugh like this, talk dirty, embarrass the laddie
when I rise to go, maternal instincts
bubble through the fug
we chasing you out, son?
silence as I click the door behind me
then laughter, warm and soft
soft as a mammy's knee

Nickin wi Chik

Used ti go nickin wi Chik.
In the Co, wan ae us liftin sherbet dips,
the other distractin the wummin.

Fae the putting green, two putters
an two baws at the ninth.
Wee Gerry seen us, says he'd tell the polis
but he'd his twinkly eye on
an we knew it was aw right
cus Gerry's a good cunt.

Stale Croissants, Edinburgh Café

A sun-blown Edinburgh morning.
She was indignant when I asked if they were yesterday's.
In a deep gaze, every moment of her life flashing
behind brown brown eyes, insisted 'No, fresh in'
so believably, with nearly yearning sadness.

Billie Holiday in the background.
No they can't take that away from me

She lied.
You could have put them on your bloody feet
walked up to the High Street, jogged,
played a game of kick the can.

But
the way she held her stare
the way she talked off key
the way I was never getting anywhere

What was that in her eyes? In one so young.
For a croissant.

Balerno Café Abomination

I'd like a decaf latte please.
With non-dairy milk.

There being only caf and no non-dairy milk
she ordered full-fat ginger beer.

Defective

Beginning, 1968

A distant thing now, in the dark of upstairs
when they were all around the fire talking
nothing more than a shudder really
and a smear of blood.
He said it would be better the next time.

*

Dykebar Hospital, 1982

Me
naked
a naked body in front of me
a towel over my arm, limp.

The worst of it is that this week
I am one of the thirds.
Three into the bathtub before the water is changed.

Her in front of me chitters
chatting and rocks her head
a brown smear on her white arse.

*

Home, 2019

I watch her leave through the eye hole.
She bends in the stairwell like a ghost.

At the window I wave.
She waves back, smiles.

The living room is magnolia.
Genna said she would help me decorate.

I go into the kitchen, the vague smell of coffee
her cup next to my cup on the bunker
a smear of lipstick on the rim.

Snowball

sharing a snowball with another person is
like dancing
twist
      and
split
      and
shimmy
      and
I hand you your half, you take it sublimely
fingers
      and
touch
      and
breath
      and

we talk about the view from the big window
wonder out to the trees and the town and the green hills

we eat it over coffee
it casts icing dust, impossible to remove

Biscuit

I put my hand out to shake the hand of Lakia,
the way I did with Hassan.
She hands me a biscuit and smiles.

It's not the culture, Hassan explains,
for a woman to shake the hand of a man.

And I think Fuckssake Lakia get a grip,
you're in a different place now,
where it's okay to shake the hand of a man.
And then I think about the kindness it was
to offer me a biscuit
to save my blushes
because I did not understand
that it is not the culture for a man to expect
to touch the hand of a woman he has only just met.

The Very Bottom of Sauchiehall Street

She stood at the bottom of Sauchiehall Street the lassie.
Vacant she was.
Stood and looked up, right over the top of the shops
stock still she was, lookin at the clouds
as they crept through blue Glasgow sky.
Least that's what I saw
when I stopped beside her and looked up
beyond the top of the buildins.
She shifted her gaze to me, smiled
and when I smiled back she said
I'm just playin.
Good that, just playin, and she had me playin along
lookin up from the street to the sky
stopped in the footfall
stopped in the middle of it all.
Playin too.

Bye, I said.
Bye, she said, and went back to lookin up.

Acknowledgements

To everyone in G2 Writers for the support that you can only find in a good writers' group: a combination of incisive crit-ique and a kick up the arse when you need it. To all the other writers I know and value for friendship, inspiration, fun; I meet so many folks with wonderful words in places of literary creativity like the Scottish Writers' Centre, St Mungo's Mirrorball, Wooer with Words, the Bakehouse in Gatehouse of Fleet.

Thanks to all who previously published many of these poems: *Poetry Scotland; Gutter; Southlight; Northwords; The Writers' Café Magazine*; Federation of Writers anthology; *Scotia Extremis; New Writing Scotland; Glasgow Just is / Justice* (ed. Linda Jackson)...

Gail Brogan who, as Pefkin, recorded Jackdaws on her Murmurations album (details...).

Tom Dalzell edited Frogs mating and Isabel mowing: thanks for a great job.

Invaluable help with German and Irish language came from Donal McLaughlin and Paul Shiels respectively: danke schön & go raibh maith agat to both.

Des Dillon for taking the time to read and review the poems. His words mean a lot and come from a writer I admire greatly.

Big thanks to Gerry Cambridge for the design and typesetting. Finally, to Sally Evans for agreeing to publish this collection, my second with Diehard. She is such an experienced writer and editor and a pleasure to work with.

Des Dillon on *Tales from the Dartry Mountains*

Charlie Gracie's poetry set in Ireland takes you directly
into the history of his family and the history of their land.
The intimacy with this land now lost in those who had to
leave. It's never directly said but those who had to leave
are now out of sorts and out of place in a land that just
doesn't quite fit them. The poem where his mother rides
a chopper bike to work describes this out of placeness
perfectly. There is a constant drone of grief for what an
immigrant loses; never again to be Irish and never quite
Scottish. And too far removed in time now anyway to
ever go back and find what is lost. The political obliqueness
and visceral descriptions are what makes these poems
work, no lectures, no diatribes and more philosophical
insight than anger.

The second part of the collection deals mostly with
Scotland (with a few trips elsewhere) and there are some
crackers in here too. It seems to me that the melancholy
of the emigrant from the Darty Mountains must bleed
into whatever Gracie writes about in the here and now.
The trace of melancholy and the longing for something
we shall never receive resonates through the whole work.
Take 'For better' for instance; a tremendously truthful look
at old age and tucked away, like a genius in Easterhouse,
is a breathtakingly exact line that could be a whole poem
itself (read it and see it). Or the T shirt for those whose
loved ones have disappeared into dementia.

A masterly, honest and melancholy collection.

A NOTE ON THE TYPE

The inner text of *Tales from the Dartry Mountains* is set in Miller, designed by Matthew Carter and released in 1997. It is a 'Scotch Roman', and follows the original style in having both roman and italic small capitals. The style was developed from types cut by Richard Austin between 1810 and 1820 at the Edinburgh type foundries of Alexander Wilson and William Miller.